The Three Little Pugs

Story Adaptation by Lauren L. Darr
Illustrations by Benacer Sipahutar

This book is dedicated to Little Mr. Zachary Tinkle.
May you always have bricks to pave your life's path.
Love Always, Mommy
(Lauren L. Darr)

Left Paw Press

Contact us on our publisher's website at:
www.leftpawpress.com

ISBN 978-0-9818360-4-1

Library of Congress Control Number: 2008911166

PRINTED IN THE UNITED STATES OF AMERICA

Story adaptations: Lauren L. Darr
Cover design and illustrations: Benacer Sipahutar

Once upon a time there was a Mother Pug with three little pugs that she loved very much.

They were very poor.

So, the Mother Pug sent the three little pugs out into the world to make homes for themselves.

Each of them went off their merry way while Mother Pug wept as they waved goodbye.

The first little pug, Benji, met a farmer with a bundle of straw, and said to him:

"Please, sir, may I have that straw to build my house?"

So the generous farmer did, and little pug Benji built his house with it.

Along came a Wolf. He knocked at the door and said, "Little pug, little pug, let me come in."

"No, no," said the little pug. "You can't come in. Not by the hair of my chinny chin chin."

"Then I'll huff and I'll puff, and I'll blow your house in," said the Wolf.

So the Wolf huffed, and he puffed, and he blew the house in.

So, little pug Benji ran as fast as he could.

The second little pug, Inky, met a lumberjack with a bundle of sticks, and said, "Please, sir, may I have those sticks to build me a house?"

So the kind lumberjack obliged, and little pug Inky built her house with them.

Along came the Wolf. He knocked at the door and said: "Little pug, little pug, let me come in."

"No, no," said the little pug. "You can't come in. Not by the hair of my chinny chin chin."

So he huffed and he puffed, and he huffed and he puffed and at last he blew the house in.

So, little pug Inky ran as fast as she could to find her siblings.

The third little
pug, Sarge, met a
masonry worker
with a load of
bricks, and said:

"Please sir, may I
have those bricks
to build me a
house?"

So, the sweet man gave him the bricks.
And little pug Sarge built his house with
them.

Soon, the Wolf came along, and said: "Little pug, little pug, let me come in."

"No, no," said the little pug. "You can't come in. Not by the hair of my chinny chin chin."

"Then I'll huff and I'll puff, and I'll blow your house in," said the Wolf.

Well, he huffed, and he puffed...

and he huffed and he puffed...

and he huffed and puffed...

But he could *not* blow the house down.

At last the Wolf stopped huffing and puffing, and said, "Little pug, I know where there is a nice field of turnips."

"Where?" said the little pug.

"On Mr. Bond's farm," said the Wolf.

"I will come for you tomorrow morning. We will go together, and get some turnips for dinner."

"Very well," said little pug Sarge, "What time will you come?"

"Oh, at six o'clock," said the Wolf.

23

Well, little pug Sarge got up at five.

He went to Mr. Bond's farm to get the turnips.

While there he found his brother Benji hiding in the field.

Little pug Sarge took Benji to his house of bricks.

Soon, the Wolf came to his house. "Little pug, are you ready?" asked the wolf.

Little pug Sarge said, "Ready! We have been and come back again. We have a nice potful of turnips for dinner."

The Wolf was very angry, but even more intrigued to think of getting two little pugs. But then he thought of another way to get the little pugs. So, he said:

"Little pugs, I know where there is a nice apple tree."

"Where?" said the pugs.

"Down in Greens Fork," replied the Wolf. "I will come for you at five o'clock in the morning and we will get some apples."

Well, the little pugs got up the next morning at four o'clock, and went off for apples.

They wanted to get back home before the Wolf came. But it was a long way to Greens Fork, and they had to climb the tree to get away from the Wolf.

Just as Benji and Sarge were climbing back down with their basket full of apples, they saw the Wolf coming!

"Little pugs!" said the wolf. "You got here before me! Are the apples nice?"

29

"Yes, very," said the little pugs. "We'll throw one down to you."

And they threw the apple as far as they could throw it.

While the Wolf ran to pick it up, the little pugs jumped down and ran home.

The next day the Wolf came again and said to the little pugs, "Little pugs, there is a fair at Darrtown this afternoon.
Would you like to go?"

"Oh, yes," said the little pugs.

"When will you come to get us?"

"At three," said the Wolf.

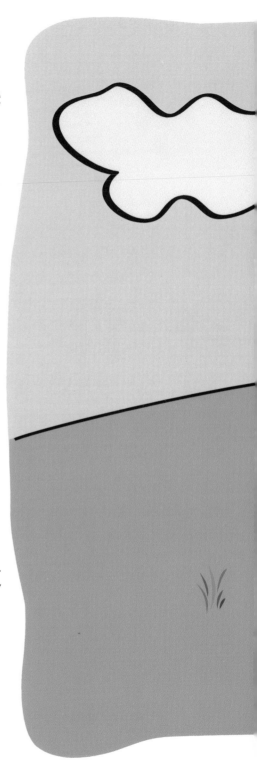

Well, the little pugs went off at two o'clock. Along the way, they met up with their sister, Inky. At the fair, they bought a butter churn. They were going home with it when they saw the Wolf coming!

The little pugs jumped into the butter churn to hide. The churn fell over and rolled down the hill. This frightened the Wolf so much that he turned around and ran home.

Later the Wolf went to the little pugs'
house and told them what happened. "A
great round thing came rolling down the
hill right at me," the Wolf said.

"Hah, we frightened you then," said the little pugs.

"We went to the fair and bought a butter churn. When we saw you, we got into it and rolled down the hill."

The Wolf was very angry indeed, but he was salivating even more at the thought of having three little pugs for dinner.

"I'm going to climb down your chimney and eat you up!" said the Wolf.

Then the little pugs heard the Wolf on the roof.

Benji hung a pot full of water in the fireplace.

Sarge built a roaring fire.

Just as the Wolf was coming down the chimney, Inky took the cover off the pot, and in fell the Wolf.

The Wolf yelled, "OUUUCCCHH!"

The three little pugs quickly put the cover back on, and boiled up the Wolf so that he couldn't harm any other pugs ever again.

And the three little pugs lived
happily ever after together
in the strong house made of bricks.

Also Available From Left Paw Press, LLC...

Mother Pug
Nursery Rhymes

Story Adaptations by Lauren L. Darr
Illustrations by Michael Elijah Cates

Also Available From Left Paw Press, LLC...

Little Red Riding Pug

Story Adaptation by Lauren L. Darr

Illustrations by Benacer Sipahutar

LaVergne, TN USA
09 December 2010
207911LV00002B